FUNNY POEMS
YOU CAN DRAW

J. C. JONES

DEDICATION

For Mum and Dad. For everything you do.

Also please draw and create in this book. I'd love to see your interpretations and so, if you like, add any you wish to my Facebook page The J. C. Jones

CONTENTS

Acknowledgments   I

1   GOD'S THRONE

2   HAPPY DOG

3   THE LUMBERJACK

4   SWEETIES

5   DRINKING BEFORE WORK

6   FEELINGS

7   STOCKBROKERS

8   THE BANK ROBBER

9   THE BIRTHDAY CAKE

10   THE ENGLISH LANGUAGE

11   THE GANGSTER

12   THE GIRAFFE

13   THE HAIRSTYLE

14   THE STRAY

15   THE SCUBA DIVER

16   THE RACEHORSE

17   THE NURSE

18   THE NEWBORN

19   THE LIFEGUARD

20   THE KITTEN

CONTENTS

21   THE JOB CENTRE

22   THE HORROR STORY

23   THE HAMSTER

24   THE JUDGE

25   THE HOUSEMATE

26   THE KING OF ANIMALS

27   THE JAILBIRD

28   THE FAMILY TREE

29   HINDSIGHT

30   THE LEARNER DRIVER

31   THE PLASTIC SURGEON

32   THE TAXIDERMIST

33   THE SWING

34   THE SHELTER

35   THE SHELL

36   WORK

37   THE TAXI DRIVER

38   THE STOWAWAY

39   THE SCHOOL MORNING

40   THE DENTIST

CONTENTS

41   ANIMALS

42   THE COACH TRIP

43   FIGHT OR FLIGHT

44   LLAMAS

45   THE DEER ARMY

GOD'S THRONE

A cat sat by God's throne and did stare,

God was a bit shocked to see him just there,

God said, "Your place here's secure,

How could you want any more?"

The cat said, "Excuse me but you're sat in my chair!"

HAPPY DOG

My dog was in a great mood today,

He was loving and so full of play,

I said, "What's made you so happy?

You're normally so snappy,"

He said, "I've just sold the cat on eBay!"

THE LUMBERJACK

There was a lumberjack called Guy,

Who only stood 3 foot high,

He never used a ladder,

As his plan it was madder,

He specialized in pruning Bonsai!

SWEETIES

A sweet shop owner loved all the sweeties,

From cola bottles to the little fizzy treaties,

He'd always eat quite a lot,

Somehow his teeth didn't rot,

However he did give himself Diabetes!!!

DRINKING BEFORE WORK

"No I can't understand the barman, not serving you anymore,

You do seem to be quite steady, as you hold onto the floor.

It probably is quite difficult, to grasp your point of view,

Especially as you are lying, at eye level with his shoe.

Yes, I agree that Tequila does really pack a kick,

But necking a whole bottle, is an awful party trick.

Of course I do believe you, that you only popped in for a few,

Apparently, you'd drank twelve pints, at just gone half past two.

I know everyone lets their hair down, and you're just cutting loose,

However you can't sober up with cider, it's alcoholic apple juice!

Yes, he's quite serious, that you do have to leave his bar,

No, he won't let you have some shots, as a last hurrah.

I do realise that it is Sunday, and it started with just a little wine,

However drinking two bottles before lunch, is very far from fine.

I understand that working on Sundays, can be a proper chore,

But let's be honest, you've done this shift many times before.

Now let's get you up and sort you out and get you back into the mix,

Come on Vicar you've a Christening to perform, that starts at half
past six!"

FEELINGS

The whole of her body became tense,

Fingers tingling feeling immense,

Next time in a field,

With a bladder to yield,

She'd double check if there was an electric fence!

STOCKBROKERS

A group of Stockbrokers tried to save their souls,

By going to the countryside on wildlife patrols,

One asked, "What tree is this?

Its' simplicity is bliss!"

Their guide said, "Ah we call them telephone poles!"

THE BANK ROBBER

A bank robber's preparations were done,

So into the bank he did run,

There was laughter and howls,

As he stood holding both barrels,

He'd sawn the wrong end off his gun!

THE BIRTHDAY CAKE

A wife was making her husband's birthday cake,

From inside as a surprise she planned to break,

But there was soon a lesson learned,

As she got herself a little burned,

Getting inside before it was cooked was definitely a mistake!

THE ENGLISH LANGUAGE

The English language does totally baffle me,

With almost every word spelt eclectically,

Getting used to the nuances can take a little time,

Words spelt so differently that somehow do rhyme.

Take rhyme for example R - H - Y - M - E,

It's not even close if you say it phonetically.

Then you have words like tough and enough,

They somehow rhyme with words like puff and bluff.

I remember learning the difference with their, they're and there,

A possessive noun, a contraction and one describing where.

Then ware, wear and where started confusing me,

I learnt they're a noun, a verb and an adverb respectfully.

It wasn't just the Homophones that caused me to despair,

There were so many other rules that I started to not care.

I recall at school learning a mnemonic rule of thumb,

I kept spelling all the exceptions wrong and feeling rather dumb,

Every child learns the simple rule I before E except after C,

After that words like weird and either didn't come easily to me,

I couldn't get my head around words like forfeit and height,

Others like seizure and foreign kept me awake at night.

When the time came for my children to start to learn,

Inside I could feel panic as my old anxiety did burn.

How could I teach them rules that I'd never understood?

If I couldn't help with their homework then who would?

I need not have worried as both are smarter than me,

And quickly they picked it all up quite effortlessly.

I watched awestruck as they took to it like flight for a fledgling bird,

When I was young I wish that I'd had spell check on Microsoft Word!

THE GANGSTER

In the Dock a Gangster did sit,

Hearing the crimes he did supposedly commit,

The Judge said, "This is a Hell of a caper,

To attack a man with sand paper!"

The gangster said, "I just roughed him up a bit!"

THE GIRAFFE

There was once a massive Giraffe called Pete,

Who for a bad neck a vet did have to treat,

As Pete stood with his head on the floor,

He said, "I've never noticed that foul odour before,

The vet said, "Why do you think your head's so far from your feet?!"

.

THE HAIRSTYLE

A lady wanted a hairstyle full of grace,

She got a Beehive as they're not commonplace,

It was fine to begin,

Until the Bees all moved in,

Now she's got Honey running all over her face!

THE STRAY

"Mrs. Jones come on through and bring your lovely hound,

Just wondering Mrs. Jones does he always make that sound?

Yes Mrs. Jones I agree he's lovely and this will be a treat,

Just wondering Mrs. Jones have you noticed his big feet?

So he's ignored all his training and does whatever he does please,

No Mrs. Jones it's not normal for dogs to be climbing trees.

Yes Mrs. Jones his teeth are very, very large indeed,

Please tell me on what exactly does little Fido feed?

I must agree Mrs. Jones he does have an enormous snout,

But everything about him is enormous, of that there is no doubt!

No I haven't ever seen a dog with that size of paws,

However I've also never seen a dog with such gigantic claws.

Yes, it is very interesting that he only ever growls,

Normally it'll be interspersed with barking and howls.

No it's not normal for dogs to raid your neighbour trash,

Nor to be hit by a car and somehow win the crash.

Oh don't worry about my assistant he often gets in a flap,

Now tell me Mrs. Jones where did you acquire this lovely chap?

You were in the woods just wandering about one day,

When you happened upon this poor, hapless stray.

Now Mrs. Jones sit down I have some news to break,

I've assessed him fully and there can be no mistake,

I must admit that I was suspicious when I first saw you in the hall,

I could see he weighed over 600 pounds and he stood eight feet tall,

You see Mrs. Jones that beast sitting there,

Is not a little doggo but a Grizzly Bear,

No being honest I don't know what to do,

My only suggestion is to take him to the zoo!

THE SCUBA DIVER

A scuba diver was on the lake's floor,

It was perfect for him to explore,

Then he found a plug,

So he gave it a tug,

Now there isn't a lake anymore!

THE RACEHORSE

There was once a racehorse called Dale,

Who was amazing but for one little fail,

The others thought it was a stunt,

As he ran back to front,

He was the first horse to ever win by a tail!

FUNNY POEMS YOU CAN DRAW

THE NURSE

My name is Bindhi I work in hospital as a nurse,
Nursing is my calling but it's also my curse.
Most of you have problems that I'll help with all day long,
But some of you are just stupid who get things rather wrong.
So you saw a YouTube clip and you thought you'd give a try,
No Mr. Smith I'm not surprised that you could not fly,
Well personally to test homemade wings if you want the truth,
I'd have jumped off a little wall and not the garage roof.
Then we have Mr. Thomas who made some terrible mistakes,
He made himself a rocket car and forgot about the brakes.
The car did over 150 which sounds like a lot of fun,
Until it wouldn't stop and he slid a mile on his bum!
Now parents here's a little tip for you on Christmas day,
Don't try out the kids presents just let the children play.
I'm fully aware that in a bygone age a long, long time ago,
That you could ride a skateboard just like you were a pro.
However times change and at your age they can cause you harm,
And it won't be a Merry Christmas when you break your arm!
Next we have do gooders raising money for a good cause,
Before you take on a challenge please just stop and pause,
I understand that raising money can seem so really cool,
But if you've not gone running since you were last in school,
Perhaps start small with a 5k walk or just a little fun run,
Because collapsing at the marathon doesn't impress anyone.
In fact a better idea and do not even hesitate,
Just sponsor someone £5 and don't participate.
Finally I come to those who do attempt some DIY,
Getting big ideas from all the tools that you can buy,
Before you buy a big chainsaw or that digger you do rent,
Think will you actually save any money after what you've spent?
I've seen the results time and again when things have gone awry,
When I've patched you lot back together after you've given it a try.
Just call a trade company off the internet or even from a book,
Because, trust me, keeping all ten fingers is a much better look!!!

THE NEWBORN

There was once a man from Llangorn,

Who could speak before he was born,

When his mums' waters broke,

The first words he spoke,

Were, "Do you mind? I was having a lie in this morn!"

THE LIFEGUARD

My name is Jason and I'm a lifeguard at the local pool,

I spend my time being handsome and generally looking cool,

I stride around the pool making that sure you don't die,

If I lose someone then my bosses would ask me why?

It's hard being a lifeguard and some people do deride,

That all I do is walk about and occasionally test the slide.

But I do so much more, many things that you do not see,

Sometimes it can take two hours to test run the Jacuzzi.

Yet I do it all like an unsung hero to get the temperature just right,

It's the same every evening as I slave away on a sunbed all the night.

My training was very difficult and nearly took up a whole week,

Learning CPR and that arm bands don't go on kiddies' feet.

Do you know the stamina it takes to flex my muscles all day long,

Standing here like an Adonis looking so beautiful and strong?

I go to the gym and I work out for an hour every day,

Just so you can look at me and feel safe in every way.

If I see you running then my whistle I shall blow,

If I blow it twice you're in trouble and you'll know!

I've worked here three years and haven't had to jump in yet,

The idea of chlorine in my hair makes me dreadfully upset,

Those of you who jump in causing quite a splash,

You know I'll produce my whistle quickly as a flash.

At least three times a day I mop the floors so they're nice and dry,

Then I'll climb my highchair for some well deserved shut eye.

Yes, there's so much to do that sometimes I just don't know where to begin,

One day when I've got the time I'm going to learn how to swim!

THE KITTEN

A cat called her kitten home as it was dark,

But she saw him playing with a mouse in the park,

She said, "Son not being rude,

You shouldn't play with your food."

He said, "It's ok mum, he identifies as a shark!"

THE JOB CENTRE

Ah Mr. Thomas thank you for being so late,

I've got nothing else to do but sit here and wait,

I can see you've been coming here for quite some time,

And your case has now officially become mine,

I've fully read your case file and it is a very sorry sight,

Every job we've sent you to they've said you're not quite right.

We've sent you on many, many courses and classes galore,

Yet you're now more unemployable than you ever were before.

Your language is awful, the way you cuss and you swear,

You're rude to everyone and it seems you just don't care.

You're the only person who has ever been fired whilst volunteering,

Do you know why the Police did suspect you of racketeering?

You can't add up and you can not spell,

You're constantly ill and feeling unwell.

You can't follow instructions on any simple task,

If you don't understand something you don't even ask,

You somehow think that you're the smartest person in the room,

But from what these reports claim you can't even use a broom.

You admit your time keeping is exceptionally poor,

And you've admitted coming here drunk many times before.

You're unemployable, a completely horrendous catch,

Yet somehow, I think I have found you the perfect match,

You won't have to travel far so do not fear,

So how would you like a job working here?

THE HORROR STORY

My blind friend was reading a book,

As I watched his fingers they shook,

I said, "What's wrong with the tale?"

He said, "It's a horror in Braille,

It's so scary my fingers daren't look!"

THE HAMSTER

Mr. Thomas was in his garden, just quietly sipping a beer,

When he became intrigued by a noise that he could hear.

Upon investigation, he located the source of the sound,

His neighbours little daughter, was digging a hole in the ground.

"That is a big hole, are you making yourself a pond?"

"No, it's for my hamster who has gone to the great beyond!"

"Oh that's very sad but unfortunately pets do die you see,

You shouldn't get attached to them, that's a rule with me.

Anyway that does not explain a hole of that size,

A hamsters not that big I hope you do now realise!"

"Ah Mr. Thomas I completely agree with all of that,

The reason the hole's so big is my hamster's in your cat!"

THE JUDGE

The accused wasn't doing too well,

The judge had a hangover from hell,

The accused burst into tears,

She was sentenced to five years,

She'd only been summoned for a bike with no bell!

THE HOUSEMATE

There's a squatter in my house but I truly don't care,

It's really quite a big house there's enough for us to share.

It's not as if anything of mine he's damaged or he's stole,

He's just a little mouse living downstairs in a hole.

THE KING OF ANIMALS

The annual meeting of all the animals was now fully in session,
Lion would be declared the king in the usual procession.
No animal dared challenge the kingdoms most ferocious beast,
Lions had ruled the kingdom for two hundred years at least!
"I am so strong and brave, and I have a fantastic mane,
To vote for anyone but me, well that would be insane!
I can swim for miles, and I can run for days,
I am the greatest animal in oh so many ways.
Is there any point in voting, or shall I just assume the crown?"
He stood on the stage looking beastly, laying his marker down.
Just as he thought they were finished, a duck walked up to the stage,
"Mr. Lion ducks are the greatest animal alive in this current age!"
All the other animals were silent, they were so amazed,
Perhaps duck had banged his head, perhaps he was dazed.
"Mr. Lion I've listened to your arguments and the points you make,
But I'm afraid to tell you that you've made a giant mistake.
You are right you are powerful, and you can run and swim,
But to think you are the greatest, your chances are quite slim."
The lion was getting angry at this challenge to his throne,
It was the greatest insult that he had ever known.
"Right my little duck friend, let's settle this once and for all,
Let's step outside this building and have ourselves a little brawl."
"Ok Mr. Lion if that's the way that it must be,
Let's go fight so that all the other animals can see."
The crowd couldn't believe what was unfolding, right before their
eyes,
Some pleaded with the duck to stop before an untimely demise.
However the duck stepped outside, and the lion followed suit,
How could such a little duck compete with such a brute?
"Right duck, this is your last chance to apologise to me,
I'm gonna start a-fighting when I count up to three!"

The duck stayed very silent and the lion he counted up to three,
The Lion started fighting as some of the crowd struggled to see.
The Lion roared and lunged at the duck with all of his might,
But when the dust had settled, the duck was not in sight.
The lion had banged his head and he had started to cry,
However the duck was safely in the air, flying in the sky.
"Mr. Lion you are great, you can run and swim like I,
Unfortunately unlike ducks, you lions cannot fly!
Duck was duly crowned, and it looked magnificent on his head,
Lions aren't kings of all animals, it's clearly ducks instead!

THE JAILBIRD

A jail bird was finally set free,

He didn't know what he should be,

His careers' advisor said, "Well,

With all the lies that you tell,

Why don't you become an MP!

THE FAMILY TREE

A man once wanted a new lover,

So he married his step mum's own mother,

Now I must confess,

His family tree is a mess,

As his grandson is also his brother!

HINDSIGHT

The older I get,

The more I regret,

The people I've lost close to me.

I've often been astounded,

Left mountain rescue dumbfounded,

Apparently, I'm the worst tour guide ever to be!

THE LEARNER DRIVER

A learner driver was taking their test,

They were nervous but trying their best,

The examiner was perturbed,

Thinking the student was disturbed,

They were so nervous they'd forgotten to get dressed.

THE PLASTIC SURGEON

A plastic surgeon got quite confused,

Leaving his patient very unamused,

The new boobs were top draw,

But there was slight flaw,

The man had come in for a hair transplant to be infused!

THE TAXIDERMIST

A taxidermist was feeling really chuffed,

After months of getting rebuffed,

She finally got a loan,

For a shop of her own,

And for all her doubters she's calling it "Get Stuffed!"

THE SWING

He stood on the seat,
Thinking this will be sweet,
His friends pushed with all of their might.
He was getting near the top,
He didn't want to stop,
The swing was now near maximum height.
There was some fear,
As the summit got near,
As the swing went flying right around,
He was cock-a-hoop,
As he did loop the loop,
And he let out a yelling sound.
He tried to hold on tight,
But something wasn't right,
And he was losing his grip on the cord.
He couldn't do a thing,
He let go of the swing,
As he realised that his plan it was flawed.
But he was feeling immense,
As he flew over the fence,
And into the garden next door.
He made his neighbour jump,
As he landed with a bump,
She hadn't seen flying children before.
Her husband wasn't pleased,
As into their garden he breezed,
And destroyed their magnificent flower bed.
"Get out of our flowers,
They're not yours they're ours,
Please try and play in your own garden instead!"
The moral of this tale,
Is try not to fail,
If you decide to make swings go full circle,
Make sure of your grip,
Try not to slip,
Because you never know where you will hurtle!

THE SHELTER

There was once a mummy from Kent,

Who found her pants all glued to a tent,

Her son said, "It's a project for school,

I think my bum shelter is cool!"

Mummy said, "I think bomb shelter is what teacher meant!"

THE SHELL

There was a man from Porthcawl,

Who was worried that he was quite small,

He once got trapped by a tide,

So in a shell he did hide,

And he was rescued by a trawler near Senegal!

WORK

A boss called an employee at home,

So he could have a whine and a moan,

He said, "I'm gonna be clear,

You only get paid when you're here,

You're a lifeguard you can't work from home!"

THE TAXI DRIVER

The Policeman simply couldn't believe his ears,

The Taxi Driver was blaming the crash on his careers,

He said, "When the passenger tapped me on the back,

I had a heart attack,

I've driven a hearse for the last fifteen years!"

THE STOWAWAY

A man fancied a holiday abroad,

But there wasn't much he could afford,

So he gave some guards the slip,

And stowed away upon a ship,

He didn't realise the Mary Rose was permanently moored!

THE SCHOOL MORNING

Wakey, wakey sleepy head, it's nearly time for school,

Stop pretending that you're ill, do I look like I'm a fool?

No you can't have five more minutes, you've snuck in ten already,

Come on, let go of the duvet and release your grip on teddy.

Right get up and brush your teeth, and you definitely need a shower,

I'll go and put your breakfast on, we've got less than an hour.

Ah there you are, your breakfast's ready, come and take a seat,

Have you forgotten something? You've no shoes upon your feet!

Let me put this bib on you, in case you spill something down your front,

It would be nice to have a conversation, all you do is sniff and grunt.

Look I know you don't want to go, it's sad for me as well,

But really you protest too much, it can't be worse than Hell!

Come on you, hurry up, you really must move much faster,

No Dad you can't skive today, you are the Schools' Headmaster!

THE DENTIST

There once was a dentist from Neath,

Who got called to a zoo about teeth,

The dentist hadn't seen this before,

The Lion had something stuck in its' jaw,

Unfortunately it was a zoo keeper called Keith.

ANIMALS

Suzie lay on the grass and watched the world go by,

The clouds all looked so fluffy high up in the sky,

"Suzie what's wrong my dear you've been an out here for an hour,

And you look like you're chewing a wasp you're looking oh so dour?"

Suzie sat bolt upright and looked squarely at her mum,

"Mother how come we're so clever and animals so dumb?"

Her mother thought for a second before sitting at her side,

She was nearly ten now and the truth she could not hide.

Softly she took her hand and smiled knowing the story she would now tell,

Her mother had told it too her long ago and the words she knew so well.

"Darling you are growing up and there's a lot for you still to see,

There are many differences between animals and you young lady,

We'll start with the easy things like how you like to dress,

Animals they just don't care they are a proper mess.

Then you wear lovely perfume and how you smell oh so sweet,

Most animals don't wash themselves going from week to week.

Our hair is also different you wear it in so many different ways,

Most animals have the same haircut until their end of days.

Suzie when you do something you always will have a plan,

Most animals just plod about and do the best they can.

Also being a lady means you're naturally eloquent and smart,

The highlight of an animal's day can be a ginormous fart.

As you get older you'll enjoy many a highbrow thing,

All an animal thinks about is dinner and drinking.

You'll also do good deeds with no masked agenda or hidden ploy,

Every time an animal gets something right you have to say 'Good boy!'

Of course the main difference between animal and us ladies,

Is we are the ones trusted to give birth to all the babies.

I mean can you imagine if your dad had given birth to you?

You'd still be inside him now and on his list of things to do!

THE COACH TRIP

A man took a coach trip to Torquay,

He said, "This is the life for me!"

So he bought himself a flat,

And thought that was that,

But his passengers were far from happy!

FIGHT OR FLIGHT

A drunk man was annoying a whole flight,

When another passenger offered him a fight,

The drunk said, "I've nothing to hide!"

As he promptly steeped outside,

And the rest of the passengers cheered with delight!

LLAMAS

A farm was being totally over run,

With Llamas attacking everyone,

The Llama herd was large,

And now that they were in charge,

Alas, finally Llamageddon had begun!

THE DEER ARMY

A group of deer invaded France,

The French army didn't stand a chance,

The French pleaded for aid,

But the World was afraid,

Everyone know you can't Pierce Deer Resistance!

ABOUT THE AUTHOR

J. C. Jones spent 25 years running pubs and nightclubs. He now spends a lot of his time writing and attempting to get his dog Spike to not eat his furniture.

FACEBOOK – THE J. C. JONES
TWITTER - @The_JCJones
INSTAGRAM - The.j.c.jones
WWW.THEJCJONES.CO.UK
EMAIL INFO@THEJCJONES.CO.UK